MAGICAL
PALETTE

Love alters all!

MAGICAL PALETTE

A Collection of Poetry and Art

Monica K. Barry

iUniverse, Inc.
New York Lincoln Shanghai

MAGICAL PALETTE
A Collection of Poetry and Art

Copyright © 2007 by Monica K. Barry

iUniverse books may be ordered through booksellers or by contacting:

iUniverse
2021 Pine Lake Road, Suite 100
Lincoln, NE 68512
www.iuniverse.com
1-800-Authors (1-800-288-4677)

ISBN: 978-0-595-41607-3 (pbk)
ISBN: 978-0-595-85955-9 (ebk)

Printed in the United States of America

To my dear family and friends

And it is only love
that makes the journey possible …—St. Eve

Contents

II   CADMIUM YELLOW

III   SAP GREEN

IV PHTHALO BLUE

V BURNT UMBER

FOREWORD

Artists are always an interesting lot. They are eclectic, introspective, and extremely sensitive to those elusive, intangible qualities that ask and answer all of those niggling questions about what it means to be a human being.

In this book of poetry, Monica K. Barry has cleverly captured the insights of an artist, the yearnings of a woman, and the compassion of a nurse. She weaves through time focusing on both the feelings of unique moments and the complex emotions that take years, if not a lifetime, to achieve.

The soul is well presented and nourished through the use of Monica's paintings and her carefully crafted words. I find this a celebration of an artful arrangement of images and words that evoke true feeling and thoughtful introspection.

It is my sincerest hope that you enjoy her work as much as I do!

Yvette M. Scholl
Author of *The Inheritance* and *The Legacy*

I

ALIZARIN CRIMSON

LOVE

I,
Who set my love upon you
With tender verve
I,
Who set my life upon you
With faith and bonding.

Want of want,
You are my lust;
Light of light,
You are my prism;
Mountain of mountain,
You are my crest;
Most of most,
You are my best.

In no other forms of love
Can I elucidate the way.
I love you.

You are the August fever of
My life
Still
As always.

O MY BELOVED

O my beloved,
Come to me
And extinguish the lamp
In my room.
Houses, trees, and the wind
Are all fast asleep.
Under the lamp, only I am awake,
Writing these lines to you.
As the light of the pale moon
Caresses my cheek coolly,
I am reminded
Of your sad eyes.
The depth of my longing for you
Is a sensual crevice,
Like fossilized bone had marrow.

O my beloved,
In this pre-dawn and velvet-soft night,
Still-glittering stars look after us,
Embracing this room.
Please, come to me,
Right here.
That we may become we,
Neither "I" nor "you."
Let us create us,
Let's be nurtured by the splendor of moon
On the beauty of flesh.

O my beloved!
My own bared winter tree!
Before morning dewdrops form
Like tears on the blades of grass,
Come to me
And extinguish the lamp
In my room.

BAILIFF

In the arms of evenfall,
In the tender tranquility
Of that kind embrace,
Hand upon hand
And heart upon heart,
Infinitely gentle,
At long last comes love.

O crescent moon,
Love's own eyebrow,
Curvature hung on the sky.
Scintillating stars
Strike the dark expanse
The silence is
A scattering of wind
Knowing and unknowing.
Finally
The moaning soul rests.

Wherever inquisitive minds waken,
This knowledge remains:
Even to muffled ears
And to closed eyes
Love comes
And loneliness dies.

YOU

You were
My love and desire
And still are.

You were
My hope and belief
And still are.

Let me justify once again:
Distance is neither crossing love
Nor breaking passion.
Longing is neither pause
Nor punishment.

There is a rooted bond
Between us;
Yes,
There always was.

SUPPLEMENT

Where
Love lies
Deeply rooted
Lovers' dreams
Secretly ferment.

Lovers bonding
Embrace life.
Where
Life is audacious,
Pride flowers
On the Earth.

Love is the soul,
Wherein
We dwell.
All promises
In harmony.

THE DISTANCE

Crossing
The Pacific
From the California
Of your thighs
To the China
Of my eyes.

There is
A course
I would chart,
A course
Of the bathymetry
Of the heart.

TIME AND LOVE

Time and love,
Being in
Short supply,
Must be stolen.
O my most lovely thief,
We must sensitize
Our fingers.
Memorize,
And never forget,
The combination
And so spring open
That vault wherein lies
Life's treasure:
Little leaves
Of love
On tiny trays
Of time.

ADVOCATE

The art of poetry requires
The poet's passionate
Presence in the line:
The crimson red ideal
Tracking the verse.
The muse dances
To the words.

Paint flows
From the heart
In tales of love.
The intensity of color,
The scent
Of the painter's pigments
Echo the painter's lines.
And the thematic content
Is but the open door
Between
The painter's eye
And the painter's passion.

Know then, beloved,
Like dripping paint,
Thoughts of you
Move across the canvas
Of my mind,
Edge to edge,
Core to core,

Each move consciously made,
None by accident,
Their fervor
As of the wild brush strokes

Such propensity
Raises no alarm,
Blinded as I am
To uncertainty
And drawn by an agony
Of yearning for you.
Therefore,
I endlessly search for
The blooming of the power
Of my artistic desire.

BLUE EYE

It is you; you looking
From a window over a wall.
The blue of your eye
Is as the glow of a sapphire.
The blue of beyond
Becomes the blue of within;
I find myself there,
Captive of your captive-seeking gaze.

And so from eye to heart
And so from heart to naked soul

Blue the eye, blood red the heart,
The soul a prism, under which
Lies dormant the ecstasies of bliss,
Twisted with dream and wanton desire
Like parched feet finding
A watered land never trod.

A THING CALLED LONGING

As hearing brings the constant sound
Of a distant hunter's horn,
So my being shoulders
A constant yoke called frailty.

And all my endeavors
As smoke from a pipe,
Curl upward in gentle air.
But heart takes hold,
And gentle becomes hurricane.

And in the silent lull
Between the storm of sound
Of rain upon rain upon rain
There is yet another constant:
In both lull and storm
A thing called longing.

THE JEWEL

Surrender to me—
No one will ever know.
I am slowly swallowing my sorrow,
Because I wish not to cry,
Because I wish not to cry again—
This I cannot bear.

Within passivity as passion
Exquisite temptation
Exquisite treasure
Exquisite wetness
Soft lips on the bare breast
As if rain empowered earth.

QUADRIVIUM

Reality is a rainbow.
Love is the prism
Through which
Its magnitude
Becomes containable,
Through which
Its waves
Become the very core
Of solitude.

NOMINALITY

Now, there is only
Remembering that memory
Having taken hold
Where what had once
Taken hold was desire:
Desperate dreams
Feverishly feeding a fire,
Like flowers in bloom
In that devoted December.
Can such grief
Be labeled grief?
Can such loss
Be labeled loss?
What, then,
Seemingly separates us?
Let what was then
Be what is now.
Remember that to you
I remain perfectly permeable,
Though reality roars,
The past purrs.

CRISIS MANAGEMENT

Beneath the willow
Rain-driven wind
Reads my bewildered mind;
Every gust telegraphing
An unspoken question:
Your eye found mine.
A moment of hesitation,
Then, you approached—
Why?
So tender the touch
But so heated the kiss
That deep in my heart,
And as forbidden
As if it were arson,
Flamed a fire of longing—
Why?

Beneath the willow
Wind-driven rain
Writes a dissolving
Memoir.
Loss is inevitable.
Everything—
All flowers,
All tears.
But one sound
Now is audible

Above the sound
Of the deluge:
The sound
Of a soft-spoken
Answer:
"I love you."

PER AMORE

In the early morning,
As the sun rises,
Thoughts of you
Bring dewdrops from my eyes.
But I know that
Where you are,
There—
There are thoughts of me.
This brings me to life.
Spring shapes,
Summer shines.
Autumn leaves fallen
From sycamore trees
Sharpen into winter.
There is one thing
That only I know:
I love you.

In the early evening,
As the sun sets,
Still I breathe
Without you.
But I close my eyes
And you are in me.
O come and
Touch my sorrow
With your tenderness.

My heart will never know
Another such love;
With no one but you
Will I ever share
Such dreams.

HABITUDE

How much do you
Want me?
How much do you
Need me?
How much do I
Fill you?
Does your heart
Overflow?

If as much as
I want you;
If as much as
I need you;
If as much as
You fill me,
Then we are divinely
Devastated,
Totally and uniquely
Inundated.

Fabulously
Chosen victims
Of the thousand-year flood
Called being.

METAPHOR

Your lips
Are as red as
Cherries.
Your smile
Is as gentle as
Your voice.
Your eyes
Are as bright as
Lightening.
Your spirit
Is as deep as
The ocean.
Your mind
Is as wide as
The sky,
Your beauty
Is the beauty
Of classical Greece
Your love
Is as close as
Your embrace.

You
Are my Aphrodite.
You
Are my enigma.

AWAKENING

"O my beloved,
What shall we eat
For breakfast?"
"O darling,
Let us eat each other,
Let us drink our passion."

Let the morning sun
Rise over
Our flaming flesh
While brilliant hummingbirds
Whirring
To engorge themselves
On the morning glories
And flame-red hibiscus
Watching us
Through the glass.

LOVESCAPE

Your presence
Is the pleasure
And to seek the savor
Of our next delicious embrace.

The joy of love
Permeates our senses
And clarifies obscurity.
The touch of love
Heightens ardor
And embellishes feeling.
The power of love
Awakens the soul
And banishes boundaries.

O selfless full abandon
Upon selfish full abundance!

Close our eyes
And visualize
In primary colors
Images of you and me—
Such a contrast,
Yet complementary.
Wrapped in wonder,
Finding our own
Pleasing rhythm,
Soothing touches,

And wanton chatter,
Waves of pleasure,
Visions from discourse
Inject ecstasy within.

DEDICATION

A restless mind,
A vibrating soul.
The fragrant scent
Of a once
Abandoned garden of love.
The gentle breeze
Of recalled touching.

Love without you is bitter,
For wild wonder is absent.
This temptation
Rules over me,
Always wishing to sin.

Untamed desire
Always approve;
Of unspoken promises,
Let them deepen.
Of unfulfilled dreams,
Act to realize them.

I don't want my wound
To be healed.
I want to be free
To know ecstasy.
I want
To show my scars.

I I

CADMIUM YELLOW

AFFIRMATION

Reaffirmed mind,
Reverberating soul.
Breathing the fragrance
Of jasmine
From once-abandoned gardens,
The skittering tickle
Of the sky's sighs,
And of memories recalled.

Love is better
Without you.
Wild wonder is gone;
That temptation
Has lost its power.
I do not wish
To stumble again.

Of untamed desires,
Let them be.
Of unspoken promises,
Let them remain.
Of unfulfilled dreams,
Let them lie buried.

I want to be rescued
Without wounds,
I want to be free
Without fears,

I want to be mended
Without scars.

O ROSE

O rose!
Such an exquisite
Contradiction!
In rhapsodic
Repose,
Arrogant
Yet humble,
Prohibitive
Yet permissive,
Each petal
Standing alone,
Yet all softly
Embrace
One another.
O rose!
O calmly curling
Crystalline
Comfort!
Fully guarded
Flamed heart,
Yet
The complete
Mystery
Beyond.

JANE

When I called your name,
You came and became
My mother.
When you called my name,
I came and became
Your daughter.

O such a bond!
O such a bridge!
You brought it to me.
I never knew it before …

You were the embodiment
Of this principle.
Your gentle charisma
Was the language
In which to read
Our love.

EXHILARATION

If I could share
A moment with you,
Would I choose
The sunrise?
The pastel sky
Over the mountain,
Or green and red
Bleeding poppy fields,
Delight of yellow butterflies
Dancing and teasing
Around fragrant flowers,
Seeking to savor attention
And waiting for approval.

Would I share
With you the present moment,
Lying across
A crisp cotton sheet?
A soft spring breeze
Caresses my body sensually,
And strokes my soul.
A moment
In time to strike
The passion,
To seek our thoughts
With our eyes.
What a gift,

The present moment
Would be to share
With you.

JUDITH SLAYING HOLOFERNES

Artemisia,
You drew yourself
By candlelight;
I drew myself
By electric light.

You are Judith,
And so am I.

Relativity within the gravity
Of a horrifying event.
Fierce aggressor's cruel crime
On a soiled sheet,
Broken the wall of purity,
The world changed forever.

But no holding back.
You became
The first recognized
Seventeenth-century
Embraced persona
In a man's world.

This painting
Is a cry,
Never to be heard again
Revenge as beauty,

Healing through art,
Justification through
The act of painting.
Tormented mind,
Finally,
Finding solace.

SUNSET

In scarlet sunset,
Suffocated
In the slanted tongues
Of hissing snakes,
In stamens of sweet blossoms,
Squirmy, scrambled dreams
Find rest at last.
In wonder,
Worry and sorrow,
Beneath the splendor
At the edge
Of consciousness,
The soul
Earns sleep.

III

SAP GREEN

SWING

Earthbound,
The swing swiftly returns
To my heaving breast,
And to my cardiac
Polydipsia.
And there—
Not in that opposite
Direction—
There it finds
That flaming
Sunset
Toward which
It is impelled.

These—
This deposition on
The nature
Of departure,
And this thirsty
And heliotropic
Supplication—
These are
The offspring
Of my Odyssey.

LIFE

Deep thoughts
Have no folds,
No flesh
To grab.
Imperative promises
Have no bounds
No soul
To touch.
Unearned knowledge
Seems sinful.
Constant doubt
Seems an effort.
Desires as habit
Become the core
Of my sorrow.
Webs of intellect
Become the shadow
Of my pride.
With no choice
Of means,
Life
Demands existence
From my limbs.

SPRING

Swiftly,
Sweetly,
Coming across
The grey sky.
Gathering warmth,
Expanding,
Mist and moisture
Come to enrich
The soft soil.
Dripping rain,
Nourishing slopes
And deep crevasses.
Soaking,
Shaking,
Lingering,
Penetrating,
And empowering
The waiting Earth.
Showering surely
So that
Roots grow,
Spring swelling.

AUTUMN

Let me bloom in autumn,
Waiting for the falling leaves to rot,
The time for luscious ripening fruit.

Let me love in autumn,
Choosing only you,
My heart's exclusive nutrient.

Let me write in autumn,
Listening to a cricket's concert.
Humble me with my own words
In long letters to old friends.

Let me be in autumn,
Understanding the soliloquy
Of a tree going bare,
Standing in solemn solitude
While restless minds
Hobble into winter.

WINTER TREE

There was never the possibility
That it would be otherwise.
Painfully taking
The freezing fury of arctic air,
The xylogenic suppuration
Impossible to stem,
The weeping winter tree stands
In utter exhaustion,
As if its very bones were bare.

The quintessential image
Of submission;
Total innocence
In total abeyance.

Pale white the winter moon,
Full bright the relentless night,
Demanding of morning sun-heat on
The blue bird's nest
By tears of frost,
Bruising the very sky.

ROTATION

Evermore
Let us live
Indigenously.

Walking along
A little creek,
Acacia flowers abloom.

In the deep green forest
The experience of …
The verdant trees,
Passionate love.

Passing rice paddies,
Learning humility
From the bending,
Full-blown head
Of ripening scented plants.

Looking at the
Winter-blue sky
Without shame,
With clean laughter,
Caressing my ears.

Evermore
Let us live
Indigenously.

CUMULUS WEB

Sunsets pass
Without a prayer.
Minds wander
Without a cry.
Treasured ideals pass
Into oblivion.
As the colors become
Dimmer and dimmer
From fringe to fringe,
Thicker and thicker
From core to core,
The consciousness
Reaches out
To grab memory.
Fragments of a dream
Honor the setting sun
With a humble kiss,
Conceiving the night
Without agitation.
Then …
Evening dies.

I V

PHTHALO BLUE

WINTER SUN

A winter of sun;
A moaning and thinning
Of bodies;
A confusion
Of wearied minds.

The solitary power
Of winter;
Wind frozen solid,
Now called
Pain.

As lips caress
A bare body,
So the fire of spring
Ignites winter's
White love.

Through the frozen fences
Of its breathing,
It hears
Its dry roots
Moaning.

EMPTINESS

Looking for words,
Mile after mile
On a bumpy road.
Out of cruise control,
Because
You chose someone else.
Who is that
Favored person?
I already had
All the words,
But I pretended
Not to know them,
Because
I am not permitted
To use them.
How unflavored are some,
And out of such depth,
How strong a cry!
So strong,
It cannot
Even be heard.
Music without sound,
Poems without words,
Plays without actors.

SEARCH

Why has only
The memory
Come to prevail,
Where passion
Once ruled us?

When I tried
To be closer to you,
You pushed me
Farther away.
When you talked
More about love,
I felt less loveliness.

Where,
Once unparalleled ecstasy
Engulfed the flesh,
Arousing and pleasing,
Vibrated the soul,
Submitting
To an evening's conclusion.

Now,
The aura of death,
The broken flowers
Abandoned in the garden,
Sobbing in regret
The vibrant colors of desire,

Painfully shackled to forget
In a white tabula rasa.

PRECIPICE

There is now
No need
To rehearse love again;
Your pleasure
Becoming my pain
Not our romance
But my remorse.
Alone and starving
On a granite-pierced clear-cut
Where once
Was a fruited paradise.
Instead of a cry for help,
Only my own
Feeble whispering.
Lord,
Let me know pain.
Let my fire
Become a frenzy
Of decaying ashes.
Let anger freeze
Passion's blazing despair.
Let desire's fury
Taste the dregs of denial.
Night-brightened,
Lust-conflagrant
Though void fuel,

Like a solar force,
Fervid and fierce.

CLIFFS

Standing alone
At Dover,
Crying alone
At the abyss,
No way forward—
Only downward.

Nothing left
But emptiness—
No flowers,
No songs,
No promises.

Now you are
Unseen,
Unscented,
Untasted,
Untouched.
Now only I hear
The lost soul
Moaning.

PROMETHEUS

Mount Caucasus,
Where man is prohibited,
Prometheus chained
To the highest peak
For being guilty
Of stealing fire
From heaven.

Under scorching sun
The tormenting ritual begins.
Wild birds
Fly in fiercely and devour
His newly grown liver
Overnight,
And it will grow
Again and again and again;
An endless ritual.

Yet
He neither sighs
Nor groans.
He has no regrets,
Nor does he seek pity
Before Zeus.
He never bends his knee
For pardon.

Days
For the tormenting test;
Nights
For the restless rest.
Prometheus chained,
Yet freed,
Prometheus suffering
His own devotion
To tormenting.

O Prometheus!
O brave Prometheus!

FAREWELL

This long separation,
No choice: an inevitability.
Why,
Why am I here?
Why am I crying?
Why,
Why are you there?
Why are you crying?
Take my hands.
Instead of crying,
Promise me again
To come to me
In my dreams;
There, we can see
Feathery flowers of our own.
There, we can hear
Voices of our own.
There, we can touch
Layers of meaning
We once shared …
I will wait for you.
I will give
Infinite simplicity,
Openly,
Exclusively,
Steadfastly.
I will blow out the candle

And leave the door
Open for you.
Where,
Where are you?
I am calling,
Calling your name.
Only the gentle moon
Calms me.
Only the cherished memories
Keep me alive.

AIDS

Frozen disease
War zone,
Beautiful young body
Eaten by demons.
Many youth
Are swept away,
Many flowers
Are lost
Before dawn.
No rules.
By nature,
The courageous
Will take
The next hill;
The cowards
Will remain
In the trench.
You must choose:
Surrender
To an arctic grave,
Or wage war
To conquer
In the spring.

THE AURA OF DEATH

Once
A planned
Rehearsal,
Now
A finished
Play.

That mad moment
Against all hopes,
Our blood racing,
Our terror and joy,
Craziness coursing
Through our brains.

Beneath reality
A slanting light
Over the expanding soul,
Constant craving
Buried
Within boundaries.

Broken love
Plummeting to stillness.
Beyond doubt
The seamless dark curtain
Slowly falling
On the empty stage.

DEPARTURE

Falling leaves
Without address
On the street.
Falling leaves
Falling,
Falling down willingly,
Until the trees
Are bare.
I cannot lose you
In autumn;
Please stay.
If you have to go,
Please leave
In winter.
Choose one snowy day
So that our white love
Will be hidden
In the snow.
While watching you go,
I will know
Where you are going
By your footprints,
And the footprints
Will become
White doves,
Flying in the sky.

EQUINOX

With the parting autumn sun,
You are cast off again.
Then, this room filled
With a warm burst
Of color, gold and glowing.
But now
I am sitting alone
And staring at
A silent silhouette,
Covered by a monochromatic
Terror and decay
Upon unkissed lips
And unsmiling eyes.
Decay of a dream,
Perception of sulfur,
Consummate
Unanswered questions
In a trembling breast.
For I must live again;
I must erase my memories
Down to the very last one
And be transformed into ashes,
Bewilder with doubt,
Be in a miracle.
A firebird will arise
From a nest of ashes,
A firebird will fiercely fly

Into empty,
Translucent sky.

V

BURNT UMBER

CODE BLUE

Code Blue!
Code Blue!

This is the zone
Of relief and misery.
This is the zone
Of truth and falsity.
This is the zone
Of the known
And unknown.

Code Blue!
Code Blue!

Modern medicine
Contests life's exit line.
Electricity tries
To revive the heart.
Shock, shock, shock.
Continue CPR,
Drug shock,
Drug shock.
Suddenly
Hemodynamic stability
Is lost again.
Nature rejects all
And triumphs at last.

The patient expires
Like a shooting star.
The torment
Is past
Without denying
Its validity.
Lights are dimmer
And dimmer …
The dream is done
Without a hero.

DNR

"Mo-mother, c-come
and-and g-get m-me."
Annie the patient
Is lamenting.
"Why am I here
Instead of holding
your hands?"
Who?
Who broke my will?
This kind of existence
I never wished.
Who?
Who took away
My right to Death?
"Mo-mother, y-you used
to s-say, *hold my hands*
when you cross troubled roads."
"Mo-mother, th-this i-is th-the t-time."
Annie the patient
Is whispering for guidance
To silence.
"Don't try to touch me,
Don't try to touch me."
Nothing is wrong
With my body
Or my soul—
Just nothing

Remains the same
Except the truth.

EXHALING

In his final breath,
His fiction unfolded.
He began the long journey
Into unknown lands.

No brain wave;
Only the young heartbeat.

All family and friends
Gathered, cried, and left,
Freeing him.
Death is the sufficient end.

Now the ventilator
Stands abandoned,
Like shining armor
Empty of its knight.

Emotional buoyancy
Transformed into silence,
All the tears
Falling into nothingness.

Before dawn,
The young flower died.
A single life entered
The void of nature
Without hesitation.

COLUMBIA: IN MEMORIAM K.C.

November 15, 2002,
We met at an art show.
You spoke softly to me
And told me your name.
Vividly I remember
Our conversation
And handshake,
Your deep, dark eyes,
Your fine, warm smile.
I knew then
What kind of person
You were.

January 16, 2003,
In the newspaper
I saw your picture;
I learned of your being
Launched into space;
I learned of you
And your background.
All of these clearly marked
The style
Of an unbridled achiever,
An undaunted explorer.

February 1, 2003,
In answering
A telephone call,
The news
Of the disaster reached me.
At once I asked myself,
"What about you?"
Flight and space
Were your passions;
Your earthly dreams
Are now done.

ART NOTES

ART IMAGE OF FRONT COVER

Title: "Multitude"
Dimensions: 16" x 20"
Oil painting on canvas by Monica K. Barry
Exhibited in the art exhibition "The Art of Harmony," curated by Hannah Bacol Busch, at the International Décor Gallery in Houston, Texas

ART IMAGE OF ALIZARIN CRIMSON

Title: "Artemisia"
Dimensions: 24" x 36"
Oil painting on canvas by Monica K. Barry

ART IMAGE OF CADMIUM YELLOW

Title: "Comfort"
Dimensions: 24" x 30"
Oil painting on canvas by Monica K. Barry

ART IMAGE OF SAP GREEN

Title: "Serenity"
Dimensions: 28" x 24"
Oil painting on canvas by Monica K. Barry

ART IMAGE OF PHTHALO BLUE

Title: "Solitude"
Dimensions: 30" x 24"
Oil painting on canvas by Monica K. Barry

ART IMAGE OF BURNT UMBER

Title: "The Aura of Death"
Dimensions: 24" x 20"
Oil painting on canvas by Monica K. Barry

To view more art @www.monicabarryfineart.com

ABOUT THE AUTHOR

Monica K. Barry has been writing poetry since her South Korean childhood, and many of her poems were published in literary journals there. She is also an artist and recently won the Lilly Oncology on Canvas International Art Competition. Barry immigrated to the United States in 1982, and she is currently a registered nurse in Houston, Texas.

978-0-595-41607-3
0-595-41607-1

Printed in the United States
85851LV00002B/13-48/A